MW00937583

The Basics Of Kanban

ADITI AGARWAL

The Basics Of Kanban

Published By: Aditi Agarwal Books LLC
Date of Publication: Oct 2018
Language: English

FREE *Membership to the Agile and Lean Leaders Mentoring Network (ALLMN)*

Be a mentor, or learn from experienced Agile and Lean leaders by subscribing to the exclusive Agile and Lean Leaders Facebook Network for Free:

Join the Facebook Group:

https://www.facebook.com/groups/AgileLeanLeaders/

Subscribe to the FREE monthly newsletter on agility and lean thinking and stay in the know!

Get an email digest of trending articles including my recent blogs to your inbox every month.

Subscribe by visiting:

https://mailchi.mp/2c566e d9e15c/newsletter

To God for his blessings
To my family for their loving support

Table of Contents

Introduction

This book is written to provide a complete and concise handbook to you such that you can familiarize yourself with Kanban and effectively manage your professional or personal work.

Who Should Read This Book?

Since Kanban can be applied at both work and your personal life, anyone can read this book. Here are a few roles and scenarios that will most likely benefit from this book.

- Project Managers
- Business Analysts
- Scrum Masters
- Product Managers
- Product Owners
- Engineers
- Test Managers
- Business Managers
- Technology Leaders
- Subject Matter Experts
- System Administrators
- Operations or Support teams
- Sales and Marketing teams

- Students seeking an IT job
- A product development team with regular intake requests
- Anyone who is looking to manage their personal or professional work
- Anyone who is looking to adopt Kanban
- Anyone who needs to understand when and when not to use Kanban
- Anyone who wants to understand the differences between Kanban and Scrum
- Anyone who needs to learn Kanban to expand one's career opportunities.
- Anyone who needs a simple and concise reference book on Kanban.

Why Did I Write This Book?

Being an Agile Coach and an experienced Scrum Master, I usually provide recommendations to the teams for practicing Scrum practices such as following a cadence, conducting Scrum ceremonies, publishing Scrum charts, writing good user stories, and so on.

Last summer, I was assigned to provide Scrum coaching to a team that was struggling to stick to a regular cadence with Scrum ceremonies. Without the ceremonies, the team lacked a good product backlog. The motivation of the team was quite low. The stories in the sprint backlog were spilling into subsequent sprints or were moving back to the product backlog. Moreover, the team had an inconsistent velocity every sprint, making it difficult to plan releases.

Considering their agile maturity, I proposed they start with the Kanban method instead. With Kanban, the team managed to streamline their intake process, minimize their in-progress/active work, gather visibility from the senior leadership, and start with standups in front of their Kanban board. They set an example for similar teams and proved that Kanban can be adapted easily with least disruption to an existing process. This encouraged other teams with similar challenges to learn more about Kanban.

A few teams reached out to me to understand core differences between Kanban and Scrum. I wanted to share a short guide with them and thus started researching into existing reference books. I came across large books on this subject and other material that cover various agile and lean methodologies. But, I was not able to find a concise handbook that can explain the complete Kanban method to busy professionals.

This book is an attempt to fill the missing gap between a 500-page detailed Kanban guide and a one-pager blog. I wrote this reference book so that you can take it anywhere you like and read whenever you want.

I hope this book will serve as a good starting point on your journey to learn Kanban. This book will also help you decide when and when not to use Kanban.

How to Use This Book?

If you are new to Kanban, I recommend that you read this book from front to back. For those who are more familiar with Kanban, you can use this book as a reference guide or a handbook.

If you are interested to compare Scrum with Kanban, jump to Chapter 8 – Scrum Vs Kanban. If you are more interested in learning Scrumban, I recommend that you read Chapter 9 – Scrumban. If you are rather interested in practical case studies on Kanban, you can start with Chapter 5 – What is a Kanban Board? and read chapters 11-15.

Ready, Set, Go

Set aside sometime each day to read and learn Kanban. The chapters that follow describe a widely used lean method to manage work effectively. Happy Reading!

Acknowledgements

First, I would like to express my gratitude to God whose blessings gave me the inspiration to write this book. I strongly believe in sharing my knowledge and helping others to succeed.

I would like to acknowledge the support of my parents who have always believed in me. Their unconditional love gave me the courage to complete this work.

This book would not have been possible without the support of my husband. I will take this opportunity to thank him for his continued support and encouragement.

Then, a special thanks to my son whose curious questions inspired me to share my knowledge and teach a complex subject in a simple manner.

I also thank my colleagues, my friends, and my mentors who trust my abilities and knowledge to write this book.

Chapter 1 – What is Kanban?

"When teams are asked to work together to analyze problems and design solutions, the quality is higher."

- *David J. Anderson, Kanban*

In 2012, I was assigned to assist a project team that was struggling to meet their deadlines. The team was overwhelmed due to the high number of quality issues or bugs and was completely stressed out. Thus, the team was unknowingly introducing new defects in the code when trying to fix the known issues. It discombobulated them increasing their anxiety, stress, and frustration. The first action that I took to mitigate the situation was to narrow down the team's focus to the top priority bugs or defects. We used to meet for 10 minutes every day to discuss the progress on the top 5 defects in the priority list. Though I didn't create a Kanban board at the time, I, unconsciously, followed a few principles and practices of the Kanban method. Today, when I reflect on that project, I comprehend that Kanban is the best approach to manage work in such situations.

Let's familiarize ourselves with the definition of Kanban and its origin in this chapter.

What Is Kanban?

Kanban is a **visual workflow management** method for managing work in an effective manner. It is a popular **lean framework** used to eliminate waste and organize work.

Kanban visualizes both the workflow process and work items flowing through the workflow. The visual representation of work items on a Kanban board allows team members to know the current state of every work item at any given time.

Kanban originally was designed for the manufacturing industry to reduce the idle time in a production process, but over time, it has become an efficient way for delivering products of **any industry**.

In a manufacturing process, Kanban covers the end to end process flow – from supplier to the end consumer. This end to end process visualization helps to avoid disruption or delays at any stage of the manufacturing process and minimizes overstocking of goods in the process.

In a traditional project management approach, developers are often overworked to complete work per the aligned plan. On the contrary, the core purpose of Kanban is to ensure a **continuous delivery** without overburdening the development team.

Kanban visualizes the flow of work items across different states thereby identifying potential bottlenecks in the process flow. Thus, with Kanban approach, the development team can proactively fix the potential impediments so work items can **continually flow** through the states at an optimal speed.

"Kanban is not a software development lifecycle methodology or an approach to project management. It requires that some process is already in place so that Kanban can be applied to incrementally change the underlying process."
– David J. Anderson

Kanban is a Japanese word that means "**visual card**" or "signboard". In the automotive sector, Kanban cards play an important role in tracking production within a factory. They signal the need to move materials within a factory. These cards also tell the supplier when to deliver a new shipment, thereby bringing **visibility** of the manufacturing process to suppliers. Kanban cards trigger a replenishment of the product or inventory based on the demand or the need of the specific product or inventory. Kanban serves as **a scheduling system** that manages what, when, and how much to produce.

Kanban is based on **just-in-time (JIT)** manufacturing principles. Just-in-time manufacturing, or JIT, is a management philosophy to eliminate manufacturing waste of finished products, half-finished products, parts, and supplies by producing only the **right amount** of parts **at the right place at the right time.** This concept minimizes the need to store inventory which adds to the cost of the product.

JIT was developed by **Taiichi Ohno** of Toyota who is now called as the father of JIT. JIT system is basically a "**pull system**" which means that the production in one system is dependent on the demand from the next system. Thus, if the next system does not need a specific part or product, it will not be manufactured. With this approach, the production of a product, or a part is completely dependent on the end user needs. This concept is also known as **on-demand production**.

Kanban facilitates the execution of a just-in-time (JIT) system by attaching visual cards or Kanban cards to every stage of a production or a process flow. Each card depicts the **quantity** and **amount of inventory** that is required to be manufactured at that stage in the production system.

Apart from JIT, Kanban is also based on **lean methodology**. This methodology aims to maximize **customer value** while **eliminating waste**. Anything that does not add value to the customer such as excessive inventory, inefficient meetings, unnecessary documentation, etc. is considered a waste. Lean focuses on eliminating such waste to continually improve the organizational system.

Kanban enables **continuous improvement** and lean concepts through a visual workflow management system and a **disciplined approach** to work. Kanban boards are visible to all stakeholders and represent a **real-time state** of work within a team or a portfolio.

Kanban cards on the board represent the actual work being completed, the assignee of the work item, and the rough estimate to complete the same in terms of hours.

To summarize, Kanban is a visual workflow management tool, or a scheduling system based on the principles of lean and just-in-time production.

Origins of Kanban

In the **early 1940s**, **Taiichi Ohno**, a Japanese industrial engineer, created a simple system to manage work and control inventory at every stage of production at **Toyota**. This production system was known as the Kanban system. Kanban was developed to achieve an efficient just-in-time production system while reducing cost-intensive waste.

"The two pillars of the Toyota production system are just-in-time and automation with a human touch, or autonomation."

— David J. Anderson

Toyota line workers used Kanban cards to send signals from one manufacturing unit to another. The **signals** denoted the need to move inventory or parts or a need to replenish materials from an external supplier into the factory. Since Kanban is based on a "pull system", each card denoted a depletion of a part or inventory and signaled **replenishment** of the same to match inventory with demand.

These cards served as **visual cues** to effectively manage their production thereby increasing quality and reducing production cost.

Like Taiichi Ohno introduced Kanban to the manufacturing industry, **David J. Anderson**, a thought leader, was the first to apply Kanban to **software development** organizations and knowledge industry in 2004. David expanded the work by Taiichi Ohno and applied a theory of constraints or a Kanban pull system on a project at **Microsoft**. In 2010, David published a book, _Kanban: Successful Evolutionary Change for Your Technology Business_ to describe Kanban and its implementation in software development.

Exercise
- What is Kanban?
- What is the difference between Kanban, JIT, and Lean?

Chapter 2 – Why Kanban?

"Predictability builds and holds trust, a core Agile value, better than does delivering more with less reliability."
- *David J. Anderson, Kanban*

In late 2014, I met a peer executive from a different organization and we had a healthy debate on adopting agile and lean methodologies vs following existing processes. His team used to manage the infrastructure requests for the entire organization. Their existing process was to meet every day to review all incoming requests and assign engineers to each of the requests. The engineer would then work on his or her assigned requests and notify all stakeholders upon completion of the request. The executive perceived the existing process as effective, except for a few outliers due to the large volume of incoming requests. Here is the conversation between us:

Me: Sounds great. How many requests are serviced by an engineer in a day?

Executive: An engineer gets assigned to around 6-10 requests per day, depending upon the volume of the incoming requests.

Me: Are all requests serviced the same day?

Executive: No, some requests get completed the same day, however, other requests may take even a week.

Me: Do engineers have visibility in each other's work requests?

Executive: They have some limited visibility into each other's work. They mostly track their own requests.

Me: How do you keep your team motivated?

Executive: Well, some engineers find it difficult to stay focused, productive, and motivated. They, typically, quit the team in a year or so.

Me: Why don't you pilot the Kanban method in your team? It will keep them **focused**, provide them **visibility** to each other's requests, and encourage them to **collaborate** with each other.

In this chapter, let's discuss the need for Kanban and its benefits, as compared to the traditional plan-driven development approach. We will also discuss when and when not to use the Kanban method.

Why Kanban?

Do you feel overwhelmed with multiple things that need your attention? Do you feel like you're always **switching** from one task to another, struggling to **focus** on any one thing for long enough to make progress? Do you feel that you work all day, but can't get anything to complete? Do you feel that you are not as productive as you would like to be? Does your team have enough **visibility** on work items that each member is working on? Does your team **struggle** to track external team dependencies? Does the team create duplicate efforts?

Kanban will help you and your team to limit the work in progress items, communicate effectively, and create visibility for the work.

Benefits of Kanban

Some of the significant benefits of the Kanban method are listed as below:

- Increased efficiency
- Improved focus
- Less waste
- Efficient communication
- Greater transparency
- Increased planning flexibility
- Fewer defects
- Continuous delivery
- Shortened time cycles

Increased efficiency:

With a traditional plan-driven approach, development team starts writing code for the requirements post design sign-off. Typically, a developer starts work on multiple tasks at the same time, switching between the tasks and trying to complete his tasks as early as possible to meet an aggressive schedule. This act of **multi-tasking** leads to less efficiency, more defects, and **low motivation**.

"You can do two things at once, but you can't focus effectively on two things at once."

- *Gary Keller*

Your efficiency is directly determined by how narrow your focus is. If you **narrow your focus** to work only on the most important task, you will complete the work more efficiently.

Kanban limits the work in progress (WIP), enabling a developer to have a **narrow focus** and **increased efficiency**.

Improved focus:
In a traditional plan-driven approach, the development team refers to the detailed requirements document and other extensive documentation to understand the scope of work items during the build phase. The massive

documentation, multiple requirements, and aggressive schedule result in reduced focus, rework, and low efficiency.

On the contrary, in the Kanban approach, the working team refers to a **visual** Kanban board with cards that provide work item description and the **current state** of the work items in the workflow. The Kanban board provides a great **visibility** into in-progress work items, thereby improving the **focus** of the working team.

"Concentrate all your thoughts upon the work at hand. The sun's rays do not burn until brought to a focus."
- Alexander
Graham Bell

Less waste:
With traditional project management approach, the development team spends several months in creating detailed requirements, design documents, and detailed plans at the start of the project, and by the time the project reaches the test phase, the requirements change, and now the team must modify the baselined

requirements, design documents, and their plans to match to the new scope of work. This results in **huge rework** and **waste**.

Kanban, on the contrary, limits the work in progress (WIP), thereby **reducing** the amount of **rework** if requirements were to change.

Moreover, Kanban board provides visibility into all work items, thus reducing **duplicate** work, conflicts, and rework.

Efficient communication:
In a traditional Waterfall approach, the **customer feedback** is received only by the time of user acceptance testing (UAT). Any change to the approved requirements during UAT results in a huge amount of waste.

On the contrary, Kanban encourages **transparency**, frequent **communication**, and alignment with the stakeholders. The Kanban board is visible not only to the team but also to other stakeholders of the effort. This promotes efficient communication, **frequent feedback**, and greater team motivation.
Greater transparency:

While there's limited transparency in the plan-driven traditional Waterfall approach, the Kanban board facilitates greater transparency of the work at any given point in time.

In Waterfall approach, each developer works on their assigned tasks and have little to no understanding about the work that is being developed by **other developers** in the team. Moreover, customers don't have any visibility on the work being developed until they see a piece of working software during the test phase.

In contrast, with the Kanban approach, one can view all the tasks and their progress displayed on a board. Everyone on the team can see **what's going on** and what each developer is working on at any moment. This promotes a greater understanding of the work being performed and increases the **collaboration** between the team.

Any roadblocks or issues within the process are visible to the entire team such that the team can take immediate action and resolve the same.

Increased planning flexibility:
With the traditional plan-driven approach, the project is strictly executed as per the **project plan** created at the start of the project. The plan is based on the aligned business needs and overall scope of the project.

On the other hand, a Kanban team pulls more work from the product backlog as they complete their WIP task. The product owner has the flexibility to **reprioritize work** in the product backlog and place the most important piece of work at the top of the backlog. This gives increased **flexibility** to the product owner and other stakeholders to adapt to changing business needs and new market conditions.

Fewer defects:
In the traditional project management approach, a developer **juggles** between multiple tasks at the same time, thereby introducing **defects** in the code. Most of the defects are uncovered during integration testing of the project. The defect fixes at that stage introduce unnecessary **rework**. It is much quicker and cheaper to fix defects at an early stage than to fix later.

On the contrary, in Kanban approach, a developer is focused only on WIP items; thereby resulting in increased focus and **reduced** number of defects. Moreover, the risk of **rework** is contained within the scope of a product increment.

Continuous delivery:
Continuous delivery (CD) is the process of releasing work to the production environment or to the end users frequently. Kanban complements the continuous delivery process as it focuses on the **just-in-time delivery** and ensures a **continuous flow** of work through the workflow process.

Unlike traditional project management approach where work is made available to end users only at the end of the project, Kanban supports the **frequent release** of work to end users, faster feedback cycle, and value delivery.

Shortened time cycles:
Cycle time is the amount of time it takes for a task to flow between different states of the workflow. In Kanban, the team drives to move the work forward through the process, thereby

shortening the cycle time. Shortened cycle time leads to a **faster time to market**.

When to use Kanban

Kanban is majorly used for the efforts that have **a continuous flow** of inbound requests. For example, consider a team that works on fixing any incoming incidents or problems raised by the end users of a specific product. Such a team will have a continuous flow of incoming requests that will flow through different states such as New, Assigned, In-Progress, Resolved, and/or Done.

Another example is of the team that solicits new ideas from product stakeholders, conducts a feasibility study, arrange for funding, and assigns an idea to a development team for building a prototype. Sample states in a workflow for this team would include 'New Idea', Business Benefits Aligned', 'Technically Feasible', 'Funds Approved', and 'Assigned to a Development Team'.

Since Kanban is simple to adapt and needs a little adjustment, it is often the **first choice** for development teams. All that is required from the team that has a queue of requests to be processed is to publish their process or workflow and set a WIP limit.

When not to use Kanban

You should not switch to Kanban if you are **not disciplined** enough to update your Kanban board regularly. If the Kanban board is not up-to-date, a developer will tend to pick up a new task from the board instead of helping other members to remove obstacles and complete in-progress tasks. The Kanban board should be treated as the main source of information.

The Kanban method will fail if the team doesn't follow **WIP limits**. If there are too many tasks that are in-progress, they will be stuck in the flow.

Another scenario where Kanban is ineffective is when it is over-engineered and **complex**. Such a board is both hard to read and difficult to update.

The below diagram (Fig. #1) represents a **sample** Kanban board that is overly complex. High complexity discourages the team to keep the board up-to-date, which is one of the core practices of Kanban.

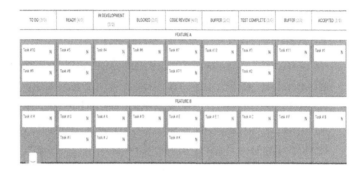

Fig. #1 A Sample Complex Kanban Board (created in the Kanbanize Tool)

Exercise
- Do you feel swamped at work or in personal life?
- What did you learn about multitasking?
- When should you use Kanban?
- When should you not use Kanban?

Chapter 3 – Kanban Principles

"Real-time flexibility beats rigid up-front planning."

- *Jim Benson, Personal Kanban*

Last month, when I had a coffee chat with my mentor, we discussed the reluctance, in general, to follow principles. If you take life itself, for example, the simple principles such as thinking positive, helping others, being compassionate, empowering others, etc. lead one to happiness and success. Almost everyone knows these principles, but people don't do what they know.

"There are three constants in life...change, choice, and principles."
- *Stephen Covey*

The core underlying principles in the Kanban method set a strong foundation for teams to adopt the same. David J. Anderson defined the **principles of Kanban** as below:

- Start with what you are doing now:
- Agree to pursue incremental and evolutionary change
- Respect current roles and responsibilities
- Encourage acts of leadership at all levels

Start with what you are doing now

The Kanban method can be applied to any **existing** process or workflow. Implementing Kanban does not signify a major change in the existing process.

Kanban does not prescribe any specific set-up to get started. Hence, this method is easy to implement in any department or group.

"Introducing a radical change is harder than incrementally improving an existing one."

- *David J. Anderson*

"Start where you are. Use what you have. Do what you can."

- *Arthur Ashe*

Agree to pursue incremental and evolutionary change

The team or the organization **must align** that the existing process or workflow needs an incremental **improvement**. In other words, the team or the department must understand that the existing process needs to be continuously improved at a slow and gentle pace.

"The first step toward change is awareness. The second step is acceptance."

- *Nathaniel Branden*

Some organizations do not adapt very well to significant or sweeping changes made to their existing processes. Such organizations or teams will adapt well to the Kanban method. Without a **need to improve** existing processes or workflows, there won't be adequate support or motivation to deploy the Kanban method.

Respect current roles and responsibilities

Implementing the Kanban method does not require any significant changes to the current roles, responsibilities, and job titles. Scrum, on the contrary, prescribes three roles to be defined – scrum master, product owner, and development team. For example, with **Scrum**, a traditional project manager will need to adapt to a **new job title** of a scrum master and its' associated responsibilities.

Kanban recognizes that there may be value in **existing processes**, roles, job titles, and responsibilities and **does not prescribe** any drastic changes to the existing structure. This eliminates any fear and makes the adoption easier.

"One of the sincere forms of respect is actually listening to what another has to say."

— *Bryant H. McGill*

Encourage acts of leadership at all levels

Anyone can be a leader. You don't need to be an executive to be a leader. This principle states that we should encourage acts of leadership at all levels within an organization, portfolio, department, or a team.

Irrespective of where one sits within an organization chart, he or she can **think strategically**, understand the big picture, collaborate effectively, and become a great leader.

"Leadership is practiced not so much in words as in attitude and in actions."

— *Harold S. Geneen*

Everyone should foster a mindset of continuous and incremental improvement to enhance their existing performance, work environment, processes, tools, and more.

Exercise

- What are the core Kanban principles?
- How do you encourage and empower others in your team?
- How will you adopt these principles?

Chapter 4 – Kanban Practices

"In Kanban, you build a map of your work. The landscape depicted is your value stream. A value stream visually represents the flow of your work from its beginning through to its completion."

-   Jim Benson,
Personal Kanban

I read a story about two first grade kids, John and Joe. It was the night before their first day to school. John was very nervous about boarding the school bus on time the next morning and was also worried about walking to the bus stop by himself at his school. He could not sleep well that night.

Joe was quite nervous too. Her father came to her room and sensed her anxiety. He enacted the entire scene with her from getting up in the morning and boarding the bus, to walking to the bus stop when school ends. Her tension eased out, and she slept peacefully that night. This story signifies that people are not distressed by the change but are intimidated by the unpreparedness of the same.

Kanban practices prepare the teams to incrementally adapt to improvements. In this chapter, we will learn popular Kanban practices and their practical applications.

The core Kanban practices are listed below:

- Visualize the flow of work
- Limit WIP (Work in Progress)
- Manage Flow
- Make Process Policies Explicit
- Implement Feedback Loops
- Improve Collaboratively, Evolve Experimentally

Visualize the flow of work

In Kanban, work is represented in a visual diagram. It is much easier to absorb and retain visual information than a written word. The **visualization of work** boosts the productivity and transparency within the team.

The Kanban board acts as a visual tool for the team and empowers them to create a **mental map** in their minds. The board is updated regularly to represent the true picture of the process.

Sample Kanban Board:

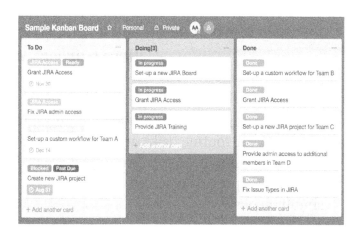

Fig. #2 A Sample Kanban Board

Limit WIP (Work in Progress)

This is the crucial aspect of Kanban. Limiting work in progress restricts multi-tasking and allows the team to pick up tasks one after another.

The key to producing extraordinary results is to concentrate on **one thing at a time**. Any story of extraordinary success, whether professional or personal, is tied to one product or service, one emotion, or one ability that drives people forward.

"There can only be one most important thing. Many things may be important, but only one can be the most important."
-   Ross Garber

Most people think that they are good at **multitasking**. The fact is though multitasking may work for routine tasks, it fails for the tasks that need brainpower. Our brains just aren't equipped to process two dissimilar tasks simultaneously.

"You must be single-minded. Drive for the one thing on which you have decided."

> -   *General George S. Patton*

Kanban encourages to **limit WIP** and narrow the focus to the tasks that are in-progress. This practice to limit WIP regulates the balance between the team capacity and incoming requests. It encourages the team to complete the work that they have started, thereby leading to greater teamwork and productivity. The team focuses on completing the ongoing work by collaborating with each other and removing obstacles.

Manage flow

The flow of work should be **fast and smooth** such that it maximizes value delivery, minimizes risk, and avoids the cost of delay. The workflow should be monitored at each stage to ensure smooth movement. Monitoring the workflow at all stages will make a system reliable and predictable. In other words, managing the workflow will **establish a**

system's cadence which, in turn, will help to determine team's capacity, thereby empowering the team to estimate how quickly a work item can be delivered.

"Let the flow manage the process, and let not the management manage the flow."

-   *Taiichi Ohno, Workplace Management*

Make Process Policies Explicit

This simply means writing up the principles and **making them visible** on the board. WIP limits are a great example of a policy wherein the team agrees to limit the in-progress work to a certain number to help work to flow through the system. The great thing about making policies explicit is that people start to **respect the policies** and understand the process better.

With a definitive and precise understanding of the process, any discussion to find improvement areas or to reduce ineffective procedures is likely to be rational, unbiased, and prudent.

Continuous improvement is a characteristic aspect of Kanban. In Kanban, people always strive to make the process better. It's a prerogative to continually improve the process by reducing inefficiencies.

In Kanban, all rules are flexible and shall be adjusted to your needs and situation.

Implement Feedback Loops

Seeking feedback is a mechanism to discover if you are on the right track or if you need to make corrections. If you get late feedback, it is likely that you have started other work which makes it harder to switch back and incorporate the feedback. In Kanban, the emphasis is given to having **short feedback loops**.

Daily standups are conducted with the team and other stakeholders in front of a Kanban board to remove impediments and ensure smooth flow of tasks. This practice assists in getting early feedback while the 'context' is still active. This is also an opportunity to assess the team's current workload and ask questions like:

- Which cards will move to done today?
- Is anyone working on anything that is not on the Kanban board?
- Is any card blocked?
- Who can unblock a blocked card?
- Are you working on more cards than defined in the WIP limit?

Weekly system demos also support early feedback from stakeholders.

"People uniformly spend too much time estimating the size, costs, and impacts of their work. They over plan up front and as context changes, they find themselves endlessly modifying their original assumptions. Planning should occur with minimal waste; it shouldn't become overhead."

- *Jim Benson,*
Personal Kanban

Improve Collaboratively, Evolve Experimentally

Kanban starts with the existing process and applies continuous and incremental improvement. This is one of the core principles of Kanban.

"Improve performance through process improvements introduced with minimal resistance."

- *David J. Anderson*

Kanban encourages an **experimental approach** where teams improve collaboratively.

Plan-Do-Check-Act (PDCA) is an effective model for continuous improvement via experimentation. In this method, the first step is to plan a change, followed by execution and testing of the change. This second step then leads to reviewing and analyzing the results.

The final step is to take corrective action based on the analysis of the results.

"It is said that improvement is eternal and infinite. It should be the duty of those working with Kanban to keep improving it with creativity and resourcefulness without allowing it to become fixed at any stage."

- Taiichi Ohno, Toyota Production System

There are several metrics that may be used to measure an improvement goal such as:

- Average WIP per person (total work in progress items for a specific period divided by the number of people in the team during that time)
- Time for which a work item was blocked
- Total number of work items completed per week or per month
- Total time taken by a work item from intake to completion.

Exercise

- What are the core practices of Kanban?
- How do you conduct your daily standup meetings?
- How do you encourage collaboration in your team?
- Think of a scenario where you can apply these core Kanban practices.

Chapter 5 – What is a Kanban Board?

"The physical board had a huge psychological effect compared to anything we got from the electronic tracking tool we used at Microsoft. By attending the standup each day, team members were exposed to a sort of time-lapse photography of the flow of work across the board. Blocked work items were marked with pink tickets, and the team became much more focused on issue resolution and maintaining flow. Productivity jumped dramatically."
- *David J. Anderson, Kanban*

A Kanban board is a **visual tool** for enabling Kanban to manage work for any business. The development teams that use Kanban leverage this board to visualize their work. The Kanban board helps a team to track each of their work items, minimize idle time, improve predictability, increase quality, and reduce time-to-market.

The board should be visible to all members of the development team such that they can closely track their tasks and dependent work items within the workflow process.

A Kanban board can be a **physical board** or **an online board**. Most teams use a physical board drawn on a whiteboard where they create one or more (swim) lanes and multiple columns to depict the different stages in their workflow process. A physical Kanban board typically uses sticky notes on a whiteboard to create a "picture" of the work. Seeing how items flow within your team's process lets you not only communicate status, but also give and receive context for the work.

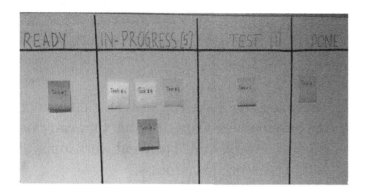

Fig. #3 A Sample Physical Board

Teams that are not co-located, or are geographically dispersed, find electronic Kanban boards better for supporting distributed teams. There are many **online Kanban tools** available in the market such as Trello, LeanKit, KanbanFlow, Kanbanize, JIRA, and more.

Trello is a web-based application which is owned by Atlassian corporation. Its Kanban boards help organize work in a fun, collaborative, and flexible way. The below diagram (Fig. #4) represents a simple Kanban board created in Trello.

Fig. #4: Trello Kanban Board

Trello allows you to add **colorful** labels to each task or work item on the board. These labels are fully **customizable** i.e. one can edit the name of the label, select the associated color, create new labels, and even delete unused ones (see Fig. #5 below):

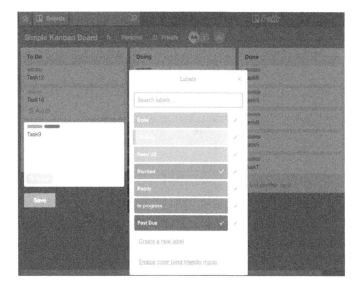

Fig. #5: Managing labels in Trello

Some of the other useful features in Trello are
that you can also add any number of additional
columns on your board, rename the default
columns, add cards to any column, define and
add labels to the cards, assign cards to your
team members, add a due date to a card, and
much more.

The main **drawback** of using Trello is the tool's inability to support Kanban **metrics** and **swimlanes**.

Another good tool to create your Kanban board is **Jira** Software. Jira is one of the best development tools used by **agile** teams to plan, track, and release great software. Kanban boards can be set-up easily within Jira. Kanban boards help your team to visualize tasks at each stage so the team can identify roadblocks, reduce cycle time, and deliver maximum value.

JIRA: https://www.atlassian.com/software/jira

Jira Software is another product from Atlassian corporation. The cloud subscription costs ~$10/month or ~$100/year for up to 10 users. Jira Software on the cloud is available for a **free trial for 7 days**. There are various plans available for server and data center hosting. Most organizations purchase **enterprise licenses** and cover their annual costs.

With Jira, you can create a new Kanban board, rename the default columns, add issues, define labels, assign an issue to a team member, link multiple issues, map an issue to an EPIC (a logical group of user stories or cards), attach a file, and much more. Below is a sample Kanban board created using Jira Software.

Fig. #6 Sample Kanban Board created using Jira Software

<u>**Kanbanize**</u> Tool is another online tool available to create your Kanban boards. It supports Portfolio Kanban Boards, **Swimlanes**, Kanban **Metrics**, Monte Carlo simulations, and much more. The 30-day trial account in **Kanbanize** provides access to all features in the system with almost no

restrictions. I leveraged its trial version to create a few sample Kanban boards for this book.

Kanbanize: https://kanbanize.com/

You can also use a Kanban board to manage your personal work. When I started to write this book, I created my personal board in Trello. The visual representation of the tasks on my personal board empowered me to **stay focused**, organize work, be productive, and remain motivated. Below is my **personal Kanban board** for authoring this book (see Fig. #7 below):

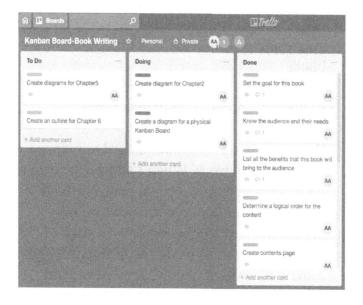

Fig. #7 Personal Kanban Board for authoring this book

Kanban boards can be used to manage any piece of work irrespective of the industry.

For example, if you are **buying a new home**, you can create a simple Kanban board and track your tasks under each column. It will help you to stay organized with your project.

Fig. #8 A Personal Kanban Sample Board for Buying a New Home

Kanban boards can be extremely **complex** too, with multiple columns and different types of activities or cards. The below section outlines a few basic **examples** of some possible Kanban board styles.

A simple Kanban board
A simple Kanban board can have three columns – To Do, Doing, and Done. Under each column, Kanban cards are placed that depict work items in different stages.

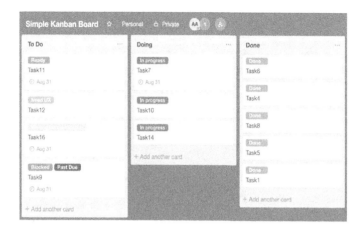

Fig. #9 A Simple Kanban Board

A time-driven Kanban board

A variation of the basic Kanban board is the board with four columns – To Do, Scheduled, In-progress, and Done. The 'Scheduled' section further slices the work items into tasks that are scheduled to start today, separating them from the ones that can start the next day.

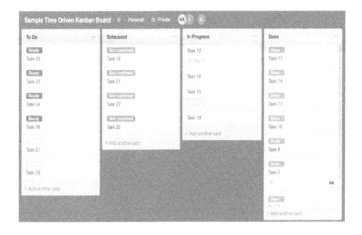

Fig. #10 A Sample Time-Driven Kanban Board

An event-driven Kanban board

In this version of the Kanban board, columns represent specific events that determine the future state of a task. This board, typically, has multiple columns depending on the number of unique events in the flow. For example, if a task cannot start until the UX design is available for the task, then the Kanban board may have a column titled 'Waiting' to segregate tasks that are not ready to be started by the team.

Fig. #11 A Sample Event-Driven Kanban Board – Example 1

Another example for an event-driven Kanban board is when the event to deploy code in the test environment triggers the subsequent action to test the change. In this scenario, the Kanban board may have an additional column titled 'Ready for Test' to segregate tasks that are ready for testing.

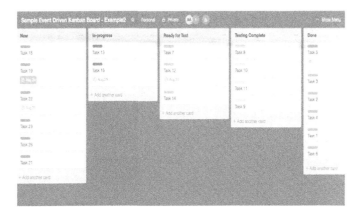

Fig. #12 A Sample Event-Driven Kanban Board – Example 2

A funding-driven Kanban board

This type of Kanban board helps to visualize different stages of a new initiative that is being approved and funded. The board can be customized in any way depending upon the stages that need to be visualized. The below diagram represents a sample Kanban board for funding approval process:

Fig. #13 A Sample Funding-Driven Kanban Board

Exercise

- Draw a Kanban board to organize your work either at the office or at home.
- Do you prefer a physical board or an online board?
- What did you learn from this chapter?

Read my blog "Kanban Boards – Practical Examples" for additional samples at:

https://authoraditiagarwal.com/2018/10/05/ kanban-boards-practical-examples/

Chapter 6 – Define WIP Limits

"It is those who concentrate on but one thing at a time who advance in this world."

- *Og Mandino*

Most successful companies have only one product or service that they are known for. For **KFC**, it started with the secret chicken recipe, for **Starbucks**, it's all about coffee and for **Google**, the one most important thing is search. **Apple**, too, focused on one product at a time, switching between Macs to iTunes to iPods to iPhones, and then to iPads.

Look around for people who live an extraordinary life. **Bill Gates** had an enormous drive for computers which led him to establish Microsoft. Similarly, **Tony Robbins**'s passion to inspire others led him to become a philanthropist, a best-selling author, and a top life strategist.

<u>It is important to comprehend the one most important goal or task that you must complete first before transitioning to the next one.</u>

One of the core properties in Kanban is that **Work in Progress (WIP)** is limited to match team's capacity. Work in Progress (WIP) Limits enforce the team to **narrow** down their **focus** to a few prioritized tasks and complete them prior to starting new ones. The lower the WIP limit the faster work will flow through the system. High WIP limits might prevent the team to discover impediments in the system.

Generally, we define WIP limit **per column**, however, it is also acceptable to define the limit **per person**. You may set the WIP limit to 1 per person working on that column. This way each person must finish their ongoing task before starting anything new. You may experiment with different WIP limits and see what works best for your team. Some teams prefer a WIP limit of 1.5 per person.

Benefits of setting a WIP limit

- Better Code Quality
- Reduces Task Switching
- Promotes Collaboration
- Increases predictability

Better Code Quality: A WIP limit guides the team to work single-mindedly on the in-progress tasks, thereby minimizing distractions and **reducing human errors**. For example, a product team of 5 engineers and 1 tester may decide to work on a maximum of 5-7 incoming enhancement requests at a time to ensure good code quality. This team does not pick up any new request until they have achieved high code coverage for their unit testing scripts, have resolved all testing defects, and have updated their automated regression test suite for in-progress requests.

"Code, without tests, is not clean. No matter how elegant it is, no matter how readable and accessible, if it hath not tests, it be unclean."

- *Robert C. Martin, Clean Code*

Reduces Task Switching: With WIP limits, **multitasking** and **context switching** is diminished. If you start something new, check emails, reply to messages on your phone or allow others to interrupt you when you are working on a task, it will take 50% more time for you to complete your task and will result in 50% more errors. With a WIP limit of 1 per person, any team member works on only one task at a time.

"When we think we're multitasking we're actually multi-switching. That is what the brain is very good at doing - quickly diverting its attention from one place to the next.

We think we're being productive. We are, indeed, being busy. But in reality, we're simply giving ourselves extra work."

- *Michael Harris*

Promotes Collaboration: WIP limits enable us to manage team capacity and collaborate with each other. If each team member is working at their maximum capacity, then they will not have any **bandwidth** to collaborate and help each other. It may mean that some team members appear underutilized. The fact is that this **slack time** provides them the opportunity to collaborate with peers, organize their work, implement continuous improvement efforts, learn new skills, or do anything else that can make them more effective at work.

"Effectively, change is almost impossible without industry-wide collaboration, cooperation, and consensus."

– Simon Mainwaring

Increases Predictability: WIP limits ensure a predictable flow of planned features that deliver value to the business. Consider the scenario when the WIP limit per person is high and engineers are working on multiple tasks at a time. They will most likely be switching contexts between tasks. Apart from that, they will be overloaded with their own tasks, will not have any time to assist others who need help, and will take more time to complete their work. With this, fewer items will move forward and the flow will be impacted.

An optimized WIP limit leaves enough room for the team to collaborate with each other, minimizes task switching, and maintains a smooth flow. An **uninterrupted steady flow** of work results in high predictability and sustainable pace.

Exercise
- Apply a WIP limit to your Kanban board
- Observe how a change in WIP limit affects the flow of work.
- Optimize your WIP limit to maximize value delivery and to have an uninterrupted flow of work.

Chapter 7 – Kanban Metrics

"If you can't measure it, you can't improve it."

- *Peter Drucker*

I remember one of the stories I read about the lasting impact that visual representations and metaphors have. In 2007, Scott Ford, CEO of the fifth US wireless provider, Alltel, announced that the company was being acquired by TPG Capital and Goldman Sachs Capital Partners. In his first meeting with the new owners, instead of a lengthy presentation, Scott presented only two slides. The first one was a picture of

Niagara Falls with a tightrope walker balanced on a cable across the width of the falls. With that picture, he conveyed the importance of having maintained a constant balance between the cash flow that the company needs to operate and the level of customer service that the company provides. The second slide was a picture of a man getting into a yellow cab on a busy NY street. He explained that waiting for the conditions to be favorable for a huge merger is like waiting for a yellow cab on the busy NY street. When a yellow cab does arrive, you better get in as you might not get another one for some time.

The one thing I learned from this story is that the **visual impact** is far greater than the impact created by any written word. Metrics, charts, or infographics too, create a similar visual impact on one's mind. They represent a large amount of information in a form of a graph or a picture.

Metrics or visual charts to represent data points such as the number of retweets, email click-through rates, number of unique visitors on the website etc. are much **easier to remember** as compared to the simple text.

Kanban provides **powerful metrics** that depict valuable workflow data. These metrics are used for continuous improvement of the production process. With the help of these metrics, a team (or process) can track their maturity over time.

There are several valuable metrics in Kanban. Some of them are listed below:

- Cumulative Flow Diagram (CFD)
- Average Lead Time Chart
- Average Cycle Time Chart
- Flow Efficiency Chart
- Blocker Clustering Chart
- Throughput Chart

Cumulative Flow Diagram (CFD)

Cumulative Flow Diagram is the visual representation of the cards as they move from one column or state to another on a Kanban board. The CFD plots the number of cards at each stage at a given time.

Below is a sample Cumulative Flow Diagram for your reference:

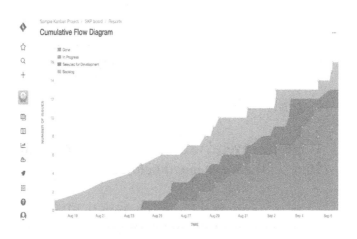

Fig. #14 A Sample CFD

The different colors on this diagram represent the various states in the flow. The height of each color band indicates the number of cards in that state at that point in time.

The CFD provides you with an insight on how many cards moved from one state to another in a specific time duration. Generally, the CFD is plotted for each day, however, if there are too many moving cards in a day, it can be plotted on an hourly basis as well. Below is a sample CFD when plotted for every hour in a working day.

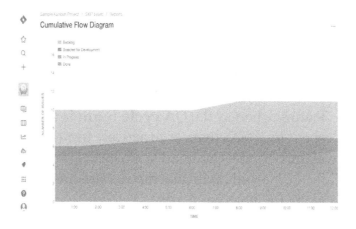

Fig. #15 A Sample CFD - Plotted Hourly

The CFD also provides valuable data on lead time and cycle time trends. Both lead time and cycle time denote the time a work item spends in the workflow until they are complete. **Lead time** is the time that a card takes from start to finish. **Cycle time** is the time an engineer spends to actively work on it.

Per the sample Kanban board illustrated in Fig. #12, the lead time is the time a card takes to flow from the 'New' column till the 'Done' column while the cycle time is the time for which a card stays in a specific column. Since cycle time can be measured for any column, it is common for several categories of cycle time to exist. For example, the **development cycle time** is the time spent by an engineer to build a feature whereas the **QA cycle team** is the time spent by a QA engineer to actively test the feature. In the Cumulative Flow Diagram, both lead time and cycle time metrics are measured along the horizontal axis.

The Cumulative Flow Diagram (CFD) also displays total cards across different columns i.e. total WIP. This data is measured along the vertical axis of the CFD diagram.

Below is a sample CFD that depicts lead time, cycle time, and the total number of cards that are in-progress (WIP) at a specific time.

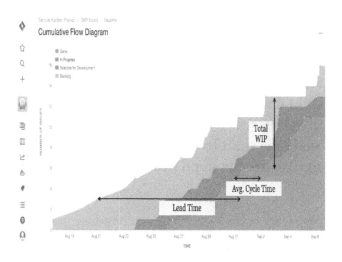

Fig. #16 A Sample CFD with Lead Time, Cycle Time, and Total WIP

Average Lead Time Chart

Average lead time is the average time taken by a work item or a card **from start to finish**. This is calculated with the **Little's Law** as below:

Average Lead Time = $\dfrac{\text{Average Work in Progress}}{\text{Average Throughput}}$

Let's consider a sample workflow where several requests or cards enter the flow each month. If the average time taken by cards to move from start to finish during the month of January is eight days, the average time taken in the month of February is five days, and so on, the average lead time chart by month, when plotted, helps to visualize the trend over time (see Fig. #17).

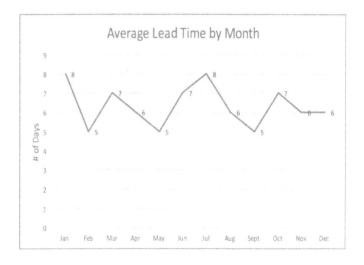

Fig. #17 Average Lead Time by Month – Sample Chart

Average Cycle Time Chart

An average cycle time chart is a visual representation of the average time taken by a work item or a card **within a specific column** or **a specific set of columns**.

Let's take the sample flow as depicted in the Kanban Chart (Fig. 9 Sample Event Driven Kanban Board – Example 2). If the average time taken by a developer to work on cards during the week is three hours, then the average development cycle time for that specific week is three hours. Similarly, if the average time for which cards remain in columns 'Ready for Test' and 'Testing' is six hours during a specific duration, then the average testing cycle time for that specific duration is six hours. These average cycle times when plotted provide **valuable insights** on the outliers and the possible bottlenecks within the flow.

The below sample chart (Fig. #18) depicts the average cycle times across four weeks.

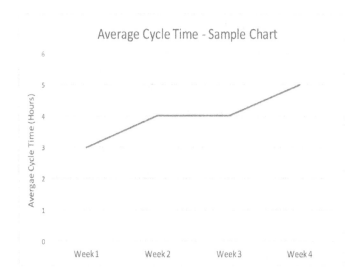

Fig. #18 A Sample Average Cycle Time Chart

Flow Efficiency Chart

Flow Efficiency (FE) is the **ratio** between the **value-added time** and the **lead time**.

Lead time is the total time from start to end of the flow. If a Kanban board has three columns – New, In-progress, and Done, then lead time is the total time taken by a card to flow from 'New' to 'Done'. Lead time comprises of wait time, block time, and active work time.

Wait time is the time for which a card is waiting on something. For example, an approval, UX designs etc. **Block time**, on the other hand, is the time for which a card is blocked due to unforeseen reasons, for example, unplanned sick days, urgent compliance issue which must be resolved immediately, or an abrupt hardware/software problem etc.

Value-added time is nothing but the active work time i.e. the time for which a card is actively worked upon.

Flow Efficiency is calculated as below:

Flow Efficiency (%) = Value-added Time/Lead Time*100

When plotted against the number of cards, this chart will provide insights into the Flow Efficiency for each card for a specific period.

Let's consider a sample where the total number of cards that enter the flow in a month is 50, out of which 20 cards have a Flow Efficiency of 60%, 10 cards have a Flow Efficiency of 50%, 15 cards have a Flow Efficiency of 90%, and 5 cards have a Flow Efficiency of only 20%. The below table represents the Flow Efficiency for different groups of cards.

# of cards	Flow Efficiency (%)
20	60
10	50
15	90
5	20

Fig. #19 Sample Data for plotting a Flow Efficiency Chart

Upon plotting the above sample data, the flow efficiency trend can be visually represented as below (Fig. #20). With this, you can identify the cards that have low Flow Efficiency and brainstorm different solutions to **minimize** any **non-value-added time**.

Fig. #20 A Sample Flow Efficiency Chart

Blocker Clustering Chart

Mike Burrows defines a blockade in his book, *Kanban From the Inside,* as:

"A blockade is an abnormal condition, that prevents already committed work from moving forward."

Blocker clustering is a technique used for identifying and grouping blockers in the flow to eliminate recurring blockers, reduce blocked time, increase throughput, and decrease the average cycle time. This technique was first developed by **Dr. Klaus Leopold**, the author of *Practical Kanban*.

First, we collect data about all blockers that occurred during a specific time duration in the workflow. Next, we capture the blocked time for each of the blockers. **Total blocked time** will help prioritize the blockers that need to be mitigated first.

It is recommended to **segregate blockers** into small groups such as waiting for more information, resource unavailability due to unplanned sick time, received an ad-hoc request with high priority, unexpected environment issues, complex defects, etc.

The higher the blocked time and the frequency of occurrence for a specific blocker, the sooner we would want a solution for the same.

Next, we leverage the scientific and proven **problem-solving techniques** such as Brainstorming, Fishbone Analysis, 5Whys, etc.

to identify potential root causes for each prioritized blocker.

If you need more information on different problem-solving techniques, you may read my other book, <u>An Expert Guide to Problem Solving – With Practical Examples.</u>

Global link: mybook.to/problem-solving-pb
US: amazon.com/dp/1539694127

This blocker clustering analysis is very effective in driving **process improvement** by reducing average cycle time and enabling faster time to market.

Throughput Chart

Throughput is defined as the **average number of items or cards** passing through the flow within a **specific time duration**.

This metric is visually represented as a histogram where the horizontal axis denotes time (in days or in months) and the vertical axis denotes the average number of cards that flow from start to finish within the time duration.

The below diagram (Fig. 21) shows a sample throughput chart for your reference.

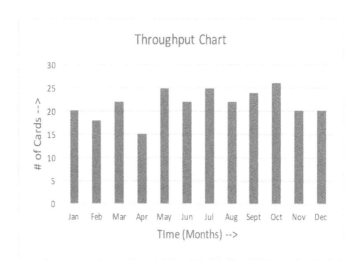

Fig. #21 A Sample Throughput Chart

Exercise

- What are the different Kanban metrics?
- Which chart did you like the most? Why?
- Did you learn anything new with this chapter?
- Measure the average cycle time and flow efficiency for your Kanban flow.

Chapter 8 – Scrum Vs Kanban

"Learn from yesterday, live for today, hope for tomorrow. The important thing is not to stop questioning."
- *Albert Einstein*

Last month, I conducted a brown bag session for senior leaders in our organization. During the discussion, I found a few experts who were tuned to Scrum methodology while others who preferred Kanban over Scrum. Due to our diverse portfolios, I could clearly understand their affinities towards one vs the other. This chapter will summarize the core differences and similarities between the two methods such that you can decide which approach works best for your team.

Scrum in a nutshell

Scrum is an iterative or incremental process framework to build **complex** products of the highest possible value.

In Scrum, the team always works on the highest priority items first. The work is performed in short, time-boxed **iterations**. Each iteration begins when the team aligns on a subset of the highest priority items that it can complete in that iteration. Each iteration ends when the team has delivered a **potentially shippable product increment** of the product. The team delivers value to the customer at the end of each iteration or a time-boxed cycle.

There are three **defined roles** – Product Owner, Scrum Master, and the Development Team. A Product Owner decides what needs to be built and in what order. A Scrum Master acts as a servant leader and coaches the team to follow Agile Scrum principles. A Development

Team is a group of self-organizing individuals who develop a high-quality product.

Scrum requires the below **ceremonies** to be conducted regularly:
- Product Backlog Refinement
- Sprint Planning
- Daily Stand-Up
- Sprint Review
- Sprint Retrospective

Scrum is most suited for complex projects where things are more unpredictable than they are predictable. In complex domains, there is a need to **collaborate** with others, have an **innovative mindset** to investigate, **experiment** with different ideas, and **adapt** based on the learnings.

To learn more about Scrum, you may read my other bestselling book, The Basics Of Scrum – A Simple Handbook to the Most Popular Agile Scrum Framework.

Global link: mybook.to/TheBasicsOfScrum-PB
US: amazon.com/dp/1521275041

Kanban in a nutshell

Kanban works best for teams that have a **continuous flow** of incoming requests with different priorities. In Kanban, each request or work item is represented by a Kanban card that flows from one stage of the workflow to another until it's complete.

Kanban is very **flexible** in nature. New work items can be added to the backlog **at any time**. Even the workflow can change anytime. If team capacity changes, WIP limits get recalibrated.

In Kanban, there is a significant focus on improving **time to market** and **eliminating waste**. The important metrics are explained in the last chapter.

Scrum Vs Kanban

The below table summarizes the core differences between Scrum and Kanban.

Scrum	Kanban
Scrum was originated for complex product	Kanban was originated to manage work and

Scrum	Kanban
development to mitigate the limitations with the Waterfall method.	control inventory at Toyota with just-in-time and lean principles.
Time-boxed and fixed length sprints	Continuous flow
Can release at the end of every sprint if required	Continuous delivery or at the team's discretion
Required roles - Product Owner, Scrum Master, Development Team	No specific roles required
The smallest piece of business value that a team can deliver in an iteration is a user story.	Each work item is represented as a Kanban card.
Scrum is best suited for complex and unpredictable efforts.	Kanban is best suited for both simple and complicated efforts where things are more predictable than they are unpredictable.
Sprint Retrospective is conducted at the end of	Service Delivery Review is conducted on a

Scrum	Kanban
every sprint to inspect and adapt the existing process.	monthly or quarterly basis to review cycle time, flow efficiency, etc.
Scrum requires user stories to be estimated in terms of story points.	Kanban does not require items or cards to be estimated. In Kanban, estimation is optional. Some teams choose to estimate their cards to have more predictability while others prefer to split their stories such that each of the cards is of the same size.
Sprint Burndown and Velocity are the key charts.	Cycle time and Throughput are the key metrics.
Less flexible	More flexible
People centric	Process centric
Scrum ceremonies are conducted on a regular cadence.	Meetings are held as needed.
Additional stories should not be added to the active/ongoing	Additional work items or cards can be added anytime, assuming it's

Scrum	Kanban
sprint.	within WIP limits.
A Scrum board or the sprint backlog is reset after every sprint.	A Kanban board is continuously used.
Requires bigger shift with roles, ceremonies, estimations, and iterations.	Nothing needs to change significantly to get started with Kanban.

Fig. #22: Comparison between Scrum and Kanban

Scrum and Kanban have many similarities too. The below list summarizes their similarities for easy reference.

- Both Scrum and Kanban are based on the **Agile Manifesto** that values:

  - Individuals and interactions over processes and tools
  - Working software over comprehensive documentation
  - Customer collaboration over contract negotiation

- Responding to change over following a plan

• Both Scrum and Kanban follow the **just-in-time** methodology. With Scrum, you create only the artifacts that you need. In Scrum, there's no need to create extensive documents such as requirements report, detailed design document, test plan, etc. that are required with the traditional plan-driven Waterfall approach. Similarly, with Kanban, only minimal documentation is created on the need basis.

• Scrum limits work in progress (WIP) in each iteration, whereas Kanban limits WIP in each column of the workflow.

• Both are empirical. Process improvements are driven via experimentation.

• Both are pull systems. Some people consider Scrum as a push system. The reason being though we pull stories into the sprint backlog based on the available capacity of the team, the stories are then pushed into the workflow (development, testing, etc.) from the sprint backlog.

- Both Scrum and Kanban encourage **collaboration** with the team.

When to use Scrum
You should choose Scrum when:

- Your organization or team needs a **massive change**.

- You need to build a **complex** and **unpredictable** product that requires innovation, research, and collaboration.

- You can conduct and attend scrum **ceremonies** on a cadence.

- You have identified people for the required Scrum **roles**.

- Your backlog consists of **different types** of **work requests** including industry research, technical feasibility study, prototyping, new feature development, iterative feature enhancements, minimizing technical debt, fixing bugs, and more.

- You have an **inconsistent flow of work** requests to your product backlog.

When to use Kanban

You should choose Kanban when:

- You have a **continuous flow** of intake requests.

- You want to optimize an **existing process** or flow of work.

- Your primary focus is to improve **speed to market** and eliminate blockers.

- You don't want any major change to **existing roles** and responsibilities.

- Your team doesn't have enough time to attend scrum ceremonies on regular cadence (this reason should not be the sole deciding factor).

Exercise

- How is Scrum different than Kanban?
- Which framework do you prefer?

To learn more about Scrum, you may read my other book, <u>The Basics Of Scrum</u> or read blogs at http://www.authoraditiagarwal.com

Global link: mybook.to/TheBasicsOfScrum-PB
US: amazon.com/dp/1521275041

Chapter 9 – Scrumban

"Intelligence is the ability to adapt to change."

- *Stephen Hawking*

<u>*This chapter is best understood by readers who have a basic understanding of Agile Scrum methodology. If you are new to Scrum, this chapter may not be relevant to you and you may want to skip to the next one.*</u>

I read a story about Ray Brooks' experience with National Car Rental company. Ray Brooks landed at Portland International Airport on Monday morning and went to National Car Rental to rent a car for his busy business trip. His first meeting was scheduled in 30 minutes.

Ray was the member of a premier club that allows frequent travelers to cut the long lines at the counter. But, when he swiped his credit card, it got rejected. Ray presented his credit card to the agent on the counter. The agent asked for his driver's license and informed Ray that his driver's license got expired last week on his birthday. Ray was shocked as he had no idea about this. The agent informed Mr. Brooks that she can't rent a car to him as he doesn't have a valid driver's license and informed her manager. The manager explained the liability that the company will have in this scenario and said, "I am sorry, but we can't rent a car to you. However, we can drive you where you'd like to go." Ray was pleasantly surprised and explained that his schedule was very hectic with meetings scheduled both in Portland and Sacramento." The manager, then, offered a creative solution to drive Ray to his first appointment, and then take him to the nearest DMV office to get his license renewed. The manager even updated the record with his new license details so that Mr. Brooks does not face any problem when renting a car in Sacramento. Ray has been a loyal customer since then.

In this story, National Car Rental provided an exceptional customer service to Mr. Brooks. They adapted their regular rental service to this unique situation, catered to the needs of their valuable customer, and set an example of an exceptional customer service for their organization.

With this story, I emphasize that one should **adapt to change** and look forward to continually improve the existing process to deliver maximum value to their customers.

Scrum and Kanban both have their benefits and drawbacks. While Scrum is best suited for product development with an inconsistent flow of different types of work items, Kanban is best suited for maintenance and support efforts with a continuous flow of intake requests.

Some development teams find it too hard to adapt to Scrum. They think it is too firm and immutable. They struggle with story point estimations, meeting their sprint commitments, and more. Often, Product Owners feel that they are over-burdened with roadmap planning, backlog refinement, prioritization, etc. At the same time, many teams find Kanban to be too lenient. Thus, **Scrumban** emerged as an Agile development methodology that is a **hybrid of Scrum and Kanban**.

In 2009, **Corey Ladas**, a software development methodology enthusiast, introduced **Scrumban** in his book, *Scrumban: Essays on Kanban Systems for Lean Software Development*. He asserts that Scrumban was created with the intent to transition a development team from Scrum to Kanban.

https://www.amazon.com/dp/B004SY63BY

Scrumban is the application of the principles of the Kanban method on top of Scrum processes. With Scrumban, we have both the familiar structure of Scrum and the flexibility of Kanban.

How to transition from Scrum to Scrumban?

To start with, you may continue to leverage Scrum practices such as sprint planning, sprint retrospective, sprint review, daily stand-up, backlog refinement, burndown charts, etc. while introducing a **Kanban board** with columns to represent different states of a user story such as New, Ready, In-Progress, Ready for Test, Testing, and Done.

You should, then, introduce the concept of **WIP limits** for each member in the team. This will limit the stories that are in progress at a given time. The team must appreciate and adhere to a simple principle of completing work before starting new work.

Each team member must work only on one work item at a time, however, if it's blocked, he or she can start work on the second item. It is not recommended to have more than 2 work items per person at a given time. In my opinion, a WIP limit of 1.5 per person works the best as it does not permit everyone to carry two work items but allows some exceptions for the blocked items.

Another change that you can introduce on your familiar Scrum process is to **delay the user story assignments** till the **last responsible moment** (LRM). The stories that are ready to be picked-up reside in the 'Ready' column on the Kanban board so that when someone becomes available, he or she should take one of the items from this list.

With the help of a Kanban board, WIP limits, and a pull-system, you are now operating as a simple Kanban on top of time-boxed sprints and scrum ceremonies. This is nothing but a **simple Scrumban**.

For **advanced Scrumban**, it's time to shift your focus on flow efficiency by leveraging Cumulative Flow Diagram (CFD), average Cycle Time chart, and average Lead Time chart instead of release and sprint burndown charts. If you have an optimized average cycle time, then your lead time will be better as well. With an optimized lead time, your flow efficiency will also increase.

Since the team now **pulls work** from the 'Ready' column, the sprint backlog will become more like a **placeholder** for containing prioritized similar-sized stories to start next.

During iteration or sprint planning, you will still pull the stories into the sprint backlog based on team's capacity and average cycle time, however, you need not break down user stories into sub-tasks and estimate each of the sub-tasks in terms of hours. This will **reduce the estimation overhead** and will simplify the sprint planning ceremony.

Consider a sample product team that writes **similar-sized** user stories and has an average **development cycle time** of 2 days. Thus, for a 2-week sprint, their engineers can work on a maximum of 5 stories each during the sprint. With a team size of 3 engineers, their sprint backlog can accommodate about 15 stories, provided the team is available for the entire sprint and does not have any planned vacation time. During the sprint planning ceremony, the team will pull the top 15 prioritized stories in the sprint backlog. This team **need not estimate** their stories in terms of story points or estimate their tasks in terms of hours.

If you must estimate your stories, consider having a **high-medium-low** estimate instead of story point estimates with planning poker.

With Scrumban, some teams prefer to reduce the sprint duration to 1 week while others tend to drop the concept of time-boxed iterations completely. The right approach depends on the problem that you are trying to solve.

Comparison with Scrum

The core differences between Scrum and Scrumban are described below:

With Scrum, the development team must have daily Scrum, backlog refinement, sprint planning, sprint review, and sprint retrospective **ceremonies** while with Scrumban, only daily Scrum is mandatory. Sprint planning, sprint review, and sprint retrospective ceremonies are optional and can be conducted as needed.

With Scrum, both user story and task level **estimations** are needed, however, with Scrumban, no estimations are needed if the user stories are of a similar size.

The main **metrics** with Scrum are Sprint Burndown and Velocity. With Scrumban, the core metrics are Cumulative Flow Diagram (CFD), Average Cycle Time, Average Lead Time, Throughput, and Flow Efficiency.

With Scrum, one cannot **add a new user story** mid-sprint. However, with Scrumban, you can add a new user story to the board anytime you want.

With Scrum, you have time-boxed **iterations** of consistent duration whereas, with Scrumban, the flow of work is **continuous**.

	Scrum	**Scrumban**
Ceremonies	All	Only daily stand-up. Others are optional.
Estimation	Yes	No (for similar-sized stories)
Metrics	Sprint Burndown and Velocity	CFD, Cycle Time, Lead Time, etc.
Changes	Wait for the next sprint	Can add anytime to the board
Iterations	Yes	Optional (as a placeholder)

Fig. #23: Comparison of Scrum and Scrumban

When to use Scrumban:

You may want to implement Scrumban when:

- You want to **add user stories** to the active sprint.

- User stories need to be **re-prioritized** during the active sprint.

- User stories **spill over** to the next sprint and you are finding it difficult to meet the time and scope constraints of Scrum.

- The team does not have **time** to attend scrum ceremonies due to busy schedules.

- The team is struggling with a story or task **estimations**.

- You have a **continuous flow** of incoming requests.

- You are doing Scrum but are interested in **Kanban** principles.

- You are **transitioning** to Kanban without causing any disruption.

- The product owner is **overwhelmed** with backlog refinement and story prioritization.

In a nutshell, Scrumban combines the structure of Scrum with the flexibility of Kanban, making it a highly versatile approach to workflow management.

Exercise

- What are the core benefits of Scrumban?
- When should you use Scrumban?

To learn more about Scrum, you may read my other book, The Basics Of Scrum or read blogs at http://www.authoraditiagarwal.com

Global link: mybook.to/TheBasicsOfScrum-PB US: amazon.com/dp/1521275041

Chapter 10 – DevOps and Kaizen

"DevOps is not a goal, but a never-ending process of continual improvement."

-   *Jez Humble*

Two years back, I was working with a scrum team that had accumulated high technical debt over the years as the team didn't have a robust automation set-up for continuous integration and continuous deployments. Thus, the team experienced quality issues, impacting their release schedule.

I met with the Product Owner and advised him to prioritize technical debt stories regarding the automation set-up. The product owner replied, "I have already committed the release date for these new features to other stakeholders. We cannot delay our release."

I advocated the importance of minimizing technical debt for the team at this stage and explained that the technical debt will increase with every new feature being released to the customers, which in turn, will lead to more defects, poor morale, and late deployments.

We finally aligned to reserve some capacity each sprint to integrate with the required tools such as Jenkins and SonarQube and to set-up our automated deployments.

We created a separate **Kanban board** with WIP limits to track this work. Every morning, we used to huddle in the front of our board to discuss the progress on each card and to mitigate blockers, if any. This method worked really well for the team and they made quite a lot of progress in a short amount of time.

What is DevOps?

DevOps is a philosophy that emphasizes the concepts of continuous integration and continuous delivery to ensure rapid delivery of quality products or services. It incorporates specific tools and techniques to enable **Continuous Integration**, **Continuous Testing**, and **Continuous Deployment**.

Why Kanban for DevOps?

Kanban is best suited for DevOps as it enables you to **visualize** your entire value-stream and ensure a stable and a **continuous** flow. It encourages teams to focus on improving the **flow efficiency** of the system.

The goals of DevOps are to integrate continuously and deploy rapidly. The ability to see progress on the Kanban board at any time empowers these goals.

Also, DevOps and Kanban work well together since Kanban is very **flexible** as compared to Scrum which is bound by time-boxed iterations.

The DevOps team usually receives multiple incoming requests at a time. The pull system of

Kanban helps the team to **focus** on one task at a time, thereby reducing the waste due to context switching and lack of priorities. The Kanban board enables the DevOps team to visualize work items and WIP limits at any time. For any new incoming request, the team gets an option to **defer or accept the request** based on the allowed WIP limit of the 'To Do' column.

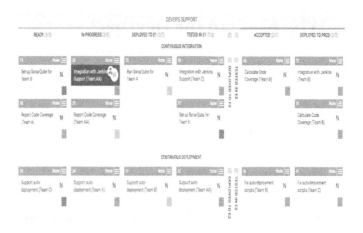

Fig. #24: A Sample Kanban Board for a DevOps Team

What is Kaizen?

Kaizen is a Japanese philosophy meaning **'continuous improvement'**. The Japanese word, itself, means ***change for better***. This ***way of life*** philosophy assumes that every aspect of life deserves to be constantly improved.

Kaizen was popularized by **Masaaki Imai** with his book *Kaizen: The Key to Japan's Competitive Success* in 1986.

https://www.amazon.com/dp/007554332X

Kaizen process is core to lean manufacturing and focuses on **eliminating waste**, **experimentation**, and **incremental improvements**. It leads to increased productivity, accountability, and morale.

The philosophy of Kaizen is that everything can be improved. It encourages the entire team to challenge the status quo, leverage **5Whys technique**, look for solutions, and make small improvements.

For in-depth knowledge on proven problem-solving techniques like 5Whys, you may read my other book, An Expert Guide to Problem Solving – With Practical Examples.

Global link: mybook.to/problem-solving-pb
US: amazon.com/dp/1539694127

Kaizen also leverages **PDCA** (Plan, Do, Check, Act) cycle to review the current state, develop a hypothesis, run experiments, evaluate results, and refine experiments for the new cycle.

The **5S framework** is another critical part of Kaizen that lays down five principles for workplace management as below:

- Seiri – tidiness or sort
- Seiton – orderliness or set in order
- Seiso – cleanliness or shine
- Seiketsu – standardized clean-up
- Shitsuke – discipline or sustain

In some areas, 5S has become 6S, the sixth element being safety.

The **Kanban** practice to <u>improve collaboratively and evolve experimentally</u> supports the Kaizen process. To make improvements or to execute Kaizen, it is important to visualize the entire process flow, elucidate the policies, and reduce the non-value-added work with the help of Kanban.

Exercise

- Why Kanban is best suited for DevOps?
- What are the similarities and differences between Kaizen and Kanban?
- How can you apply the 5S framework?
- How can you share your learnings with others in your family or team?

Kanban Case Study#1

"Simply put, things always had to be in a production-ready state: if you wrote it, you darn well had to be there to get it running!"

-   *Mike Miller*

Let's consider a scenario that a DevOps team receives several requests each day to automate build process in Jenkins, resolve environment issues, run automated code reviews via SonarQube, onboard new applications onto a hybrid cloud, and so on.

Here's a sample Kanban board for such a scenario (see Fig. #25):

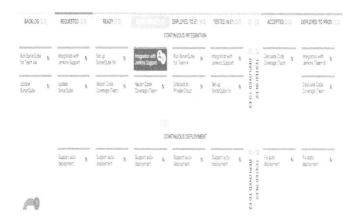

Fig. #25: A Sample Kanban Board for Case Study#1

The key highlights for the above sample Kanban board are as below:

- Separate swimlanes for *Continuous Integration* and *Continuous Deployment* to manage work effectively
- Multiple columns on the board to visually represent and track the flow of testing across test environments.

- WIP limit has been applied to the column 'In Progress'
- A blocked card in column, 'In-Progress'

Exercise

- What changes will you bring to the sample Kanban board?
- Does this case study apply to your team or portfolio?
- How do you manage DevOps work in your organization?
- How should this sample DevOps team minimize its blockers?

Read my blog "Kanban Boards – Practical Examples" for additional samples of Kanban Boards at https://authoraditiagarwal.com

https://authoraditiagarwal.com/2018/10/05/ kanban-boards-practical-examples/

Kanban Case Study#2

"Perfection is not attainable, but if we chase perfection, we can catch excellence."

- *Vince Lombardi*

Let's consider a scenario that an operations team receives several calls during the day from its customers and works together to analyze reported issues, provide real-time guidance, and execute fixes to a customer-facing application.

Below diagram represents a sample Kanban board for such a scenario (see Fig. #26):

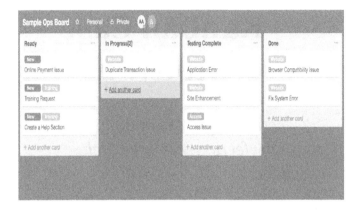

**Fig. #26: A Sample Kanban Board for
Case Study#2**

The key highlights for the above sample Kanban
board are as below:

- Different colors or categories tagged to the
  cards to identity the type of request e.g.
  training, access, website, etc.
- Simple board with few columns to track the
  work efficiently
- No use of swimlanes
- WIP limit set for only one column
- No Backlog or To Do column
- No buffer for blocked cards

Exercise

- What changes will you bring to the sample Kanban board?
- Does this case study apply to your team or portfolio?
- Which online tool do you prefer to create your Kanban boards?

Read my blog "Kanban Boards – Practical Examples" for additional samples of Kanban Boards at https://authoraditiagarwal.com

https://authoraditiagarwal.com/2018/10/05/ kanban-boards-practical-examples/

Kanban Case Study#3

"Success today requires the agility and drive to constantly rethink, reinvigorate, react, and reinvent."
- *Bill Gates*

Let's consider a scenario that a software development team receives new requests on a regular basis to build new capabilities and enhance existing application features. This team targets to deliver a quality code and invests time in peer code reviews and application testing.

The below diagram represents a sample Kanban board for such a team (see Fig. #27):

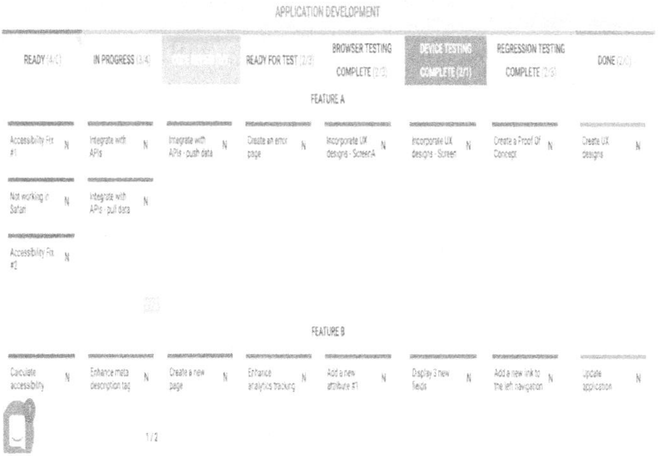

Fig. #27: A Sample Kanban Board for Case Study#3

The key highlights for the above sample Kanban board are as below:

- Separate swimlanes for segregating work across different features of the product
- Multiple columns on the board to track the flow of cards across different types of testing such as Browser Testing, Device Testing, and Regression Testing

- WIP limits have been applied to multiple columns including 'Code Review'. The WIP limit for the 'Code Review' column depends on how many people in the team are reviewing the code. Lack of a WIP limit for this column usually overwhelms the code reviewers and results in cards being blocked.
- The WIP limit has exceeded on the 'Device Testing Complete' column.
- Color scheme for cards in different states

Exercise

- What changes will you bring to the sample Kanban board?
- Does this case study apply to your team or portfolio?
- Did you learn anything new with this board?

Read my blog "Kanban Boards – Practical Examples" for additional samples of Kanban Boards at https://authoraditiagarwal.com

https://authoraditiagarwal.com/2018/10/05/kanban-boards-practical-examples/

Kanban Case Study#4

"It is not the strongest of the species that survives, nor the most intelligent, but the one most responsive to change."
- *Charles Darwin*

Let's consider a scenario that an organization's legal team receives requests on a regular basis from different portfolios in the organization to review content on their sites, campaigns, offers, etc. from a legal point of view. The number of requests that they receive is so high that it becomes difficult for them to track the incoming requests, conduct legal reviews, and respond to the requesters in a timely manner.

If I were to create a Kanban board to manage work for such a team, it would look like the sample Kanban board below (Fig. #28).

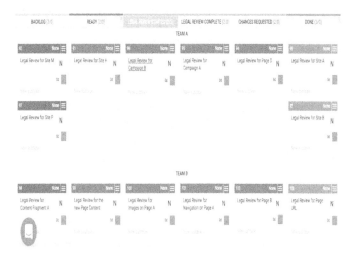

Fig. #28: A Sample Kanban Board for Case Study#4

The key highlights for the above sample Kanban board are as below:

- Separate swimlanes for segregating work requests from different teams
- Specific columns on the board to represent and track the legal review workflow
- The WIP limit has exceeded on the 'Legal Review Started' column.
- Color scheme for cards in 'Backlog' and 'Done' columns to differentiate these from other columns

Exercise

- What changes will you bring to the sample Kanban board?
- Does this case study apply to your team or portfolio?
- Did you learn anything new with this board?

Read my blog "Kanban Boards – Practical Examples" for additional samples of Kanban Boards at https://authoraditiagarwal.com

https://authoraditiagarwal.com/2018/10/05/ kanban-boards-practical-examples/

Kanban Case Study#5

"We cannot make informed decisions or create a quality product without first understanding why we are doing what we are doing."

- *Jim Benson*

Let's consider a scenario that a platform team receives multiple requests from different application teams every day to onboard their applications onto the new platform.

The below diagram (Fig. #29) denotes a sample Kanban board for such a team.

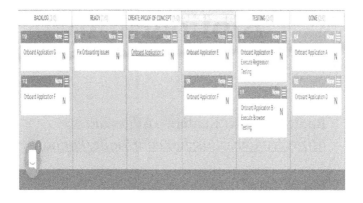

Fig. #29: A Sample Kanban Board for Case Study#5

The key highlights for the above sample Kanban board are as below:

- No use of swimlanes
- Custom columns to represent and track the application onboarding workflow
- Color scheme for cards in 'Backlog' and 'Done' columns to differentiate from others
- The WIP limit set for a single column

Exercise
- What columns will you define for this sample Kanban board?
- What will be your WIP limits?

Bibliography

Radigan, Dan. "Kanban". Atlassian.
https://www.atlassian.com/agile/kanban

Evans, Gareth. "Kanban Lead and Cycle Time - Why So Important?". Kanban Tool. Kanban Library. 2009-2018.
https://kanbantool.com/kanban-library/analytics-and-metrics/kanban-lead-and-cycle-time

Unknown. "Kanban for Engineering". LeanKit. Planview. 2018.
https://leankit.com/learn/kanban/kanban-for-engineers/

Unknown. "Using Kanban for DevOps and Continuous Delivery". Digite. 2018.
https://www.digite.com/kanban/kanban-for-devops/

About Me

Aditi Agarwal provides Agile coaching to help teams develop complex products effectively. Being a certified SAFe Program Consultant (SPC), a certified Scrum Master (CSM), and a certified Project Management Professional (PMP), she has a proven track record of delivering high-value products and services. She is very excited to share her knowledge with her readers. Her mission is to spread knowledge, positivity, love, and compassion in the world.

Aditi lives in Phoenix, AZ with her loving family. Aditi writes short books in a straight-forward and an easy-to-understand language such that readers can derive maximum value without investing time in reading bulky books.

More Books by the Author

1. _The Basics Of Agile and Lean: Develop an Agile Mindset and Lean Thinking_

   This book is written to introduce you to the core values and principles of both **Agile** and **Lean** methodologies.

   Global link: mybook.to/AgileandLean-Paperback

   US: amazon.com/dp/108124741X

2. _The Basics Of SCRUM: A Simple Handbook to the Most Popular Agile Scrum Framework_

   This book explains the **Scrum** roles, artifacts, ceremonies, and principles, along with advanced concepts such as managing technical debt, writing good *user stories, publishing scrum charts, and more. The Basics Of Scrum will be useful to those who want to learn Scrum and expand their career opportunities, or those who don't have time to read bulky books and thus need a simple reference book on Scrum.*

Global link: mybook.to/TheBasicsOfScrum-PB

US: amazon.com/dp/1521275041

3. *Enterprise Agility with OKRs: A Complete Guide to Achieving Enterprise Business Agility*

Enterprises must achieve "true agility" to sustain businesses and drive outcomes in this fast-paced, competitive, and rapidly changing environment.

This book is specially designed for thought leaders who are leading agile transformation efforts, coaching agile or lean frameworks, implementing OKRs, or bringing more business agility to their enterprise.

Global link:
mybook.to/EnterpriseAgility-PB

US: amazon.com/dp/1087285119

4. *An Expert Guide to Problem Solving –*
   With Practical Examples

   *This book will give you an understanding of the different problem-solving tools such as **Fishbone Diagram, Brainstorming, Failure Modes and Effects Analysis, SWOT matrix, and 5Whys** along with practical examples and applications of these tools.*

   Global link:
   mybook.to/problem-solving-pb

   US: amazon.com/dp/1539694127

5. *Emerging Technology Trends:*
   Frequently Asked Questions

   *This book covers frequently asked questions about emerging technology trends such as **Blockchain, Bitcoin,***

Ethereum, Ripple, Artificial Intelligence, Machine Learning, Artificial Neural Networks, Deep Learning, Augmented Reality, Connected Homes, Quantum Computing, *and more. Read today and stay in the know!*

Global link: mybook.to/EmergingTrends-PB

US: amazon.com/dp/1980821291

6. *Harness The Power Within: Unleash your Inner Strength with Faith, Patience, and a Positive Mind*

The purpose of this book is to inspire you to live a happy and a fulfilled life. You can overcome any obstacle in life by unlocking the powers contained within you. There's a famous quote, "We are never defeated unless we give up on God."

Global link: mybook.to/HarnessPowerWithin-PB

US: amazon.com/dp/1544783825

7. _Embrace Positivity: Think, Speak, and Act – A 3-Step Strategy to Live Your Best Life_

*This motivational **self-help** book reveals a 3-step strategy to embrace **positivity** in life. It emphasizes the role of positive thinking, affirmations or the spoken word, and positive actions in attaining self-esteem and success. This book can be used as a handbook or a reference book to achieve success through a positive mental attitude.*

Global link: mybook.to/EmbracePositivity-PB

US: amazon.com/dp/1659810566

Don't forget to subscribe to the **FREE** monthly newsletter on agility and lean thinking!

Get an email digest of trending articles including my recent blogs to your inbox every month.

To subscribe, enroll here: https://mailchi.mp/2c566e d9e15c/newsletter

Post your review

*If you found any value with this book, please submit your **honest review** on Amazon. Your review will help me to improve the content of this book and reach a wider audience.*

***Special Thanks** for your encouragement and continued support.*

*Check out my **website**: https://authoraditiagarwal.com*

Made in United States
North Haven, CT
06 August 2023

40015413R00078